PSYCHOEDUCATIONAL GROUP CURRICULUM AND ACTIVITIES GUIDE

Carmichael Finn

PSYCHOEDUCATIONAL GROUP CURRICULUM AND ACTIVITIES GUIDE

To every individual who has ever walked through the doors of treatment with trembling hands and a heavy heart—this workbook is for you.

It is for the brave souls learning to trust themselves again, for the parents striving to heal while raising the next generation, and for the countless people in recovery whose stories are often misunderstood, minimized, or unseen. You are not your past. You are not your worst day. You are worthy of recovery, of peace, and of belonging.

To the clinicians, counselors, peers, and group facilitators who hold space day after day—often while carrying your own invisible burdens—thank you. This work is demanding, sacred, and life-altering. May these pages offer you tools, structure, and compassion to make your work just a little lighter and a lot more impactful.

To my fellow helpers, educators, and leaders who dare to believe that healing is possible even in systems that sometimes feel broken—thank you for choosing this path. Your hope matters.

For Sarah.

With humility and hope,

Carmichael Finn, MA, LMFT, LADC
Carmichael Finn LLC

First Printing, 2025

ISBN/SKU: 979-8-9991858-0-8
EISBN: 979-8-9991858-1-5

Disclaimer:

This workbook is intended for use by licensed clinicians and professionals trained in group facilitation. It is not a substitute for individualized clinical assessment, medical treatment, or therapy. Please consult appropriate professionals for diagnosis and care.

Psychoeducational Group Curriculum and Activities Guide: for Substance Use Disorder Treatment

Carmichael Finn MA, LMFT, LADC, ADCR-MN

Introduction

This *Psychoeducational Group Curriculum and Activities Guide* is designed for use in substance use disorder treatment programs to provide structured, evidence-informed, and therapeutically engaging sessions across a 13-week curriculum. Each weekly group explores a key theme relevant to substance use recovery—from understanding the cycle of addiction to building relationships, managing emotions, and fostering self-efficacy.

Facilitators are provided with clear objectives, discussion prompts, facilitation tips, and experiential activities to promote client insight, peer connection, and real-world application. The guide integrates trauma-informed, harm-reduction, and strengths-based approaches, making it adaptable for diverse clinical settings and client needs.

Cumulative Learning Objectives:

1. Increase awareness of addiction patterns, triggers, and relapse cycles.
2. Build coping and emotional regulation skills using practical, evidence-based techniques.
3. Improve relationship functioning through healthy communication, boundary-setting, and pro-dependent frameworks.
4. Enhance mindfulness, self-esteem, and self-compassion as protective factors in recovery.
5. Develop life skills in financial management, time organization, and nutrition to support holistic well-being.
6. Foster a supportive peer community where lived experiences can be shared, validated, and transformed into recovery capital.

How to Use

How to Use This Curriculum

This workbook is designed as a practical, flexible resource for clinicians facilitating psychoeducational groups in behavioral health and substance use disorder treatment settings. It can be used as a **stand-alone curriculum** or as a **modular supplement** to existing programming. Each weekly topic is structured to support continuity, therapeutic engagement, and client learning while remaining adaptable to the clinician's personal facilitation style.

Clinician Preparation

Before each group, clinicians are encouraged to:

Review the week's content and objectives thoroughly to understand the focus and learning goals.

Read the referenced materials and supplemental readings where available. These were chosen to deepen your knowledge and expand your clinical framework when teaching the topic.

Review the Clinician's Notes for the week, which provide expanded facilitation tips, language considerations, activity adaptations, and important cultural and clinical insights.

Familiarize yourself with the group worksheets, as many include space for reflection, journaling, or activity completion that may require guided support or additional explanation.

Flexibility and Clinical Judgment

This curriculum is **intentionally adaptable**. The activities and scripts are offered as tools, not mandates.

Clinicians are encouraged to:

Modify or expand exercises based on group dynamics or time constraints.

Substitute or integrate material with other evidence-based approaches you already use (e.g., DBT, CBT, Seeking Safety, MI).

Adjust language, examples, or tone to align with your population's needs, cultural context, and developmental level.

Your clinical insight and relational presence are the most important tools in delivering this content effectively. The workbook was designed with the understanding that **no two facilitators, clients, or programs are alike**—and that's a strength.

Language choices, group process, and worksheet prompts are built with trauma-informed care in mind. Facilitators are encouraged to maintain **a tone of curiosity, non-judgment, and empowerment** throughout the program.

How Clients Learn

Clients may be at different stages of readiness, learning, or recovery. This curriculum honors that. Some may engage deeply with worksheets; others may benefit more from listening, drawing, or sharing verbally. **All participation is valid.** Provide clients space to interact with the content in a way that honors their recovery process.

Licensing & Distribution

This content is the intellectual property of Carmichael Finn, LLC and is meant for use in therapeutic, educational, or programmatic settings by trained facilitators. For licensing questions, bulk distribution, or adaptation inquiries, see the copyright page.

Group One: Understanding the Cycle of Addiction

Group One: Understanding the Cycle of Addiction

Summary: Explore the stages of addiction and the factors that contribute to the cycle.

Objectives:
- Identify the stages of addiction.
- Recognize personal triggers and patterns.
- Develop awareness of how to break the cycle.

References: "The Stages of Change" by Prochaska & DiClemente.
Supplemental Reading: "In the Realm of Hungry Ghosts" by Gabor Maté.

How to Facilitate:

- - Start with an explanation of the addiction cycle.
- - Use visual aids (e.g., diagrams).
- - Discuss real-life examples.

Activities:

- - Have clients draw their own cycle of addiction.
- - Facilitate group sharing.

Language Matters: Reducing Stigma with Client-Centered Terms

When presenting the addiction cycle, it's important to acknowledge that the word *relapse* can feel harsh, shaming, or final to many clients. For some, it carries the weight of failure or disappointment, which may inadvertently discourage openness or reinforce internalized stigma. An alternative term—*recurrence of use*—is increasingly recognized in clinical and recovery spaces for its nonjudgmental tone and accuracy. It frames substance use as a chronic, relapsing condition with ups and downs, rather than a moral failing.

As a facilitator, consider using both terms during group discussions. You might say, *"Some people use the word relapse, others prefer recurrence of use—use whichever feels right to you."* This invites client autonomy, models compassion, and fosters a safer environment for exploration. Ultimately, the goal is to support clients in understanding their patterns—not label them for slipping.

Clinician's Notes: Group One

Clinician's Notes: Group One

Clinician's Preparation & Core Knowledge

Before facilitating this session, it's important that you have a strong grasp of both the Addiction Cycle and the Stages of Change Model. The addiction cycle typically includes a repeating pattern of emotional trigger → substance use → short-term relief → negative consequences → guilt/shame → craving → preoccupation → and back to the beginning. Understanding how this cycle sustains itself biologically, psychologically, and socially will help you guide the group toward deeper insights.

Also familiarize yourself with the Stages of Change Model (Prochaska & DiClemente), which frames recovery as a dynamic and nonlinear process:

1. Precontemplation
2. Contemplation
3. Preparation
4. Action
5. Maintenance
6. Relapse/Recurrence

Reading or reviewing Gabor Maté's work (especially his focus on trauma, attachment, and emotional pain as the root of addiction) will help you shift the tone of the group from 'What's wrong with you?' to 'What happened to you?' This fosters compassion and invites vulnerability.

Essential Talking Points for Clients

- "Addiction is not a moral failing, but a learned survival loop." This reframes addiction from a shame-based narrative to one of patterned behavior that can be disrupted.
- "Everyone's addiction cycle is unique." While the core pattern is consistent, the triggers, emotions, and consequences vary. Help clients see themselves as experts in their own experience.
- "Awareness is power." Understanding how addiction shows up in your life is the first step toward reclaiming control.

- "Recovery is not a straight line." Use the Stages of Change to show that relapse doesn't erase progress—it's part of the process for many.

Engagement Tips to Make This Group Come Alive

- Start with energy and curiosity. Say something like: "Today we're going to look at addiction not as something that makes you broken—but as a pattern that you've learned to survive. And patterns can be unlearned."
- Use a large printed diagram of the addiction cycle or draw it together. Make it visual and collaborative.
- Encourage creativity. When clients draw their own addiction cycle, normalize variation. Offer colored pencils and ask them to label emotions, events, or images that represent their personal experience.
- Invite curiosity, not confession. Emphasize that sharing is optional, and that reflection is still participation. Some clients will connect internally without speaking much.
- Create connection moments. Ask: "How many of you noticed guilt or shame showing up in your cycle?" or "Did anyone see something in their drawing they didn't expect?" These questions prompt organic discussion.

Final Word to the Clinician

Group One sets the emotional tone for the entire curriculum. If you can help clients leave this session feeling seen, understood, and empowered—even just a little—you've done your job. Keep the group strength-based, normalize ambivalence, and remind them that learning their own patterns is not only possible but deeply hopeful. This week is about planting seeds of self-awareness that future sessions will help grow.

Identify Your Personal Cycle

Group ONE: Worksheet One

Relapse/Recurrence Cycle Exploration Worksheet

This worksheet is designed to help you explore your personal patterns related to relapse/recurrence or near-relapse/recurrence. Understanding your relapse/recurrence cycle can empower you to interrupt it and develop healthier coping strategies.

Think about a time you relapsed, recurrence of use or came close to using. Reflect on the stages that led up to it.

TRIGGERS: What internal or external triggers showed up? (e.g., emotions, stress, people, places, events)

THOUGHTS: What were you telling yourself in those moments? (e.g., 'I can handle one', 'It's not a big deal')

URGES & FEELINGS: What cravings or emotional states did you notice? How intense were they?

BEHAVIORS: What actions did you take (or avoid)? (e.g., stopped going to meetings, isolated, lied)

USE OR CLOSE CALL: Describe what happened. If you used, what did that look like? If not, what stopped you?

CONSEQUENCES: What were the short- and long-term impacts on your physical, emotional, and relational wellbeing?

REFLECTION: Looking back, what might you do differently now with the tools you have?

Part 2: Visualize Your Cycle

Use the space below to draw your personal relapse/recurrence cycle. You can use arrows, boxes, or symbols—whatever helps you understand the flow of your thoughts, feelings, and behaviors. Include what happens before, during, and after the moment of use or near-use.

[Draw your cycle below or use a separate sheet of paper if needed]

Part 3: Interruption Points

Now that you've explored your cycle, identify points where you can intervene to stop the cycle from continuing.

• What are 3 signs that you're entering your relapse/recurrence cycle?

• What are 3 tools or supports you can use to disrupt your cycle?

• Who can you reach out to when you notice the early warning signs?

• What is one new coping strategy you want to try when you're feeling triggered?

You can bring this worksheet to your next group or individual session if you'd like support exploring it further.

The Six Stages of Change

Group ONE: Worksheet Two

Stages of Change: Self-Assessment Worksheet

This worksheet is designed to help you reflect on where you are in your recovery journey. The Stages of Change model shows that change happens over time and through different phases. Each stage is valid and important. This tool will help you identify your current stage and consider some helpful next steps.

1. **Precontemplation:** You're not yet thinking seriously about change or don't believe change is needed.

2. **Contemplation:** You're aware a problem exists and are considering making a change, but feel unsure or ambivalent.

3. **Preparation:** You're getting ready to take action and may have already made small changes.

4. **Action:** You're actively working on changing behaviors and building new habits.

5. **Maintenance:** You're continuing with the changes you've made and working to avoid slipping back.

6. **Recurrence of Use:** You've returned to old behaviors. This is part of the process—not a failure.

Self-Assessment: What Stage Am I In?

Answer the following questions to help determine your stage:

1. Do you think your substance use is causing problems in your life? Why or why not?

2. Are you thinking about making a change in your use?

3. Have you tried to make changes recently? What did that look like?

4. What support or tools have you used to help with change?

5. If you've had a recurrence of use, how did you respond afterward?

What to Focus On Based on Your Stage

Use the guide below for suggested goals or focus areas based on your current stage.

Precontemplation Stage

- Explore how your use affects different areas of your life.
- Talk to someone you trust about their observations.
- Learn about addiction and recovery without pressure to change.

Contemplation Stage

- Weigh the pros and cons of changing your use.
- Journal about your fears and hopes around change.
- Attend a group or session just to listen and learn more.

Preparation Stage

- Set a small, manageable goal related to reducing use.
- Identify people or resources who can support you.
- Plan for potential triggers or challenges.

Action Stage

- Stay connected to your support network.
- Track your progress and celebrate small wins.
- Use coping tools and revisit your motivation regularly.

Maintenance Stage

- Reinforce routines that keep you grounded.
- Prepare for high-risk situations and create a safety plan.

- Consider how you can support others or give back.

Recurrence of Use Stage

- Reflect without judgment—what happened and what can you learn?
- Reconnect to support immediately.
- Set a new small goal and re-engage with your recovery plan.

Final Reflection

Change is a process. Wherever you are, it's okay. Use this worksheet to reflect and return to it as you grow. Bring it to your next group or individual session to discuss your insights and goals.

Group Two: Coping Skills Toolbox

Summary: Teach clients practical coping skills to manage cravings and stress.

Objectives:
- Learn at least three new coping strategies.
- Create a personalized toolbox of skills.

References: DBT Skills Training Handouts and Worksheets by Marsha Linehan.
Supplemental Reading: "The Dialectical Behavior Therapy Skills Workbook" by McKay, Wood, & Brantley.

How to Facilitate:
- Discuss the importance of coping skills.
- Provide examples.

Activities:
- Have clients create a list of skills they can use.
- Role-play scenarios to practice skills.

Note: This session draws from Dialectical Behavior Therapy (DBT), developed by Marsha Linehan. For full materials and skills training handouts, see Linehan, M. (2015). DBT Skills Training Manual (2nd ed.).

Clinician's Notes: Group Two

Clinician's Preparation & Core Knowledge

Group Two centers on equipping clients with practical tools to manage distress without returning to substance use. Grounded in Dialectical Behavior Therapy (DBT), this session introduces core coping skills such as distraction, self-soothing, grounding, and opposite action. These skills help clients tolerate emotional discomfort and resist impulses by increasing their behavioral repertoire.

Review DBT's Distress Tolerance and Emotion Regulation modules in advance, especially the 'ACCEPTS' and 'IMPROVE' mnemonics, and be ready to translate clinical language into real-world application. Emphasize that coping skills are not one-size-fits-all; clients should experiment and personalize what works for them.

Also understand that clients may arrive with shame or internalized failure from past coping failures. This session should emphasize trial-and-error, encouragement, and the concept of a 'toolbox' as something we build over time.

Essential Talking Points for Clients

- "Recovery isn't about always feeling good—it's about having the tools to cope when you don't."
- "Coping skills are like tools. You won't use a hammer for every job, and you won't use the same skill for every feeling."
- "What worked once may not always work again—and that's okay. Keep building your toolbox."
- "There is no shame in needing a plan to get through tough moments. That's strength, not weakness."

Engagement Tips to Make This Group Come Alive

- Start by asking the group what they usually do when they're stressed or triggered. Normalize both helpful and unhelpful responses.

- Bring in visual aids like a printed DBT skills handout or a sample 'Coping Toolbox' filled with items (stress ball, soothing scent, grounding card, etc.).

- Model vulnerability by sharing a time when a coping strategy helped you—or when you had to try multiple tools before one worked.

- Avoid jargon. Translate clinical DBT terms into accessible language (e.g., 'opposite action' becomes 'doing the opposite of what your urge says').

- Create energy by turning the role-play into a 'coping challenge': present stressful scenarios and let the group brainstorm different responses.

- Encourage creativity: Coping skills can include music, movement, connection, sensory input, or spiritual practices. Let clients think outside the box.

Final Word to the Clinician

Coping skills are the scaffolding clients will lean on when they're tempted to return to use. This session is less about perfect execution and more about experimentation, empowerment, and flexibility. Reinforce that building a coping toolbox is a lifelong process—not a one-and-done task. Celebrate client creativity, normalize trial and error, and remind them: Every skill practiced is one more brick in the foundation of long-term recovery.

Coping Skills List

Group TWO: Worksheet One

100 Coping Skills: Self-Reflection Worksheet

Coping skills are strategies and actions you can take to manage stress, emotions, cravings, and everyday challenges. Below is a list of 100 coping skills. Read through the list and circle or highlight the ten that feel most useful or appealing to you.

Then, complete the reflection section for each of your chosen coping skills. This will help you think through how these skills can be used in your life and how things might change if you actually practiced them consistently.

1. Take a walk
2. Listen to music
3. Journal your thoughts
4. Call a friend
5. Deep breathing
6. Drink a glass of water
7. Draw or color
8. Watch a funny movie
9. Practice yoga
10. Meditate
11. Do a puzzle
12. Dance
13. Write a letter you don't send
14. Take a shower or bath
15. Read a book
16. Clean a space
17. Squeeze a stress ball
18. Play a game
19. Go outside

20. Sit in the sun
21. Hug a pet
22. Exercise
23. Stretch
24. Cook something new
25. Organize your closet
26. Listen to a podcast
27. Volunteer
28. Plant something
29. Create a playlist
30. Do a random act of kindness
31. Drink tea
32. Sing loudly
33. Write poetry
34. Take a nap
35. Use essential oils
36. Practice gratitude
37. Say affirmations
38. Write down five strengths
39. Plan a fun activity
40. Use grounding techniques
41. Visualize a safe place
42. Use a fidget toy
43. Talk to a counselor
44. Use a coping box
45. Plan your day
46. Learn something new
47. Set a small goal
48. Watch a sunset
49. Stargaze
50. Journal what you're grateful for
51. Write a recovery letter
52. Declutter
53. Color a mandala
54. Attend a support group
55. Learn a breathing pattern
56. Make a vision board
57. Name your emotions
58. Listen to nature sounds
59. Make your bed
60. Write a forgiveness letter

61. Practice progressive muscle relaxation
62. Start a hobby
63. Light a candle
64. Pray or reflect spiritually
65. Use positive self-talk
66. Do a crossword
67. Journal about triggers
68. Research something inspiring
69. Watch an inspiring TED Talk
70. Speak kindly to yourself
71. Identify one small thing you can control
72. Track your mood
73. Use coloring books
74. Laugh
75. Practice assertiveness
76. Take a break from social media
77. Write a goodbye letter to addiction
78. Join an online recovery forum
79. Say no to something draining
80. Practice letting go
81. Keep a feelings log
82. Practice DBT skills
83. Paint or sculpt
84. Knit or crochet
85. Make a gratitude jar
86. Pet an animal
87. Use aromatherapy
88. Memorize a quote
89. Create an emergency plan
90. Make a self-care checklist
91. Try guided imagery
92. Listen to binaural beats
93. Spend time with supportive people
94. Go somewhere new
95. Do a digital detox
96. Take five deep belly breaths
97. Use humor
98. Read recovery literature
99. Schedule something to look forward to
100. Practice saying what you need

Reflection Section

Pick ten coping skills from the list. For each one, complete the following:

Coping Skill #1

1. What skill did you choose?

2. Why do you think this skill might work for you?

3. When could you use it in your life?

4. How would using this skill make your life different?

5. What might get in the way of using it—and how can you plan around that?

Coping Skill #2

1. What skill did you choose?

2. Why do you think this skill might work for you?

3. When could you use it in your life?

4. How would using this skill make your life different?

5. What might get in the way of using it—and how can you plan around that?

Coping Skill #3

1. What skill did you choose?

2. Why do you think this skill might work for you?

3. When could you use it in your life?

4. How would using this skill make your life different?

5. What might get in the way of using it—and how can you plan around that?

Coping Skill #4

1. What skill did you choose?

2. Why do you think this skill might work for you?

3. When could you use it in your life?

4. How would using this skill make your life different?

5. What might get in the way of using it—and how can you plan around that?

Coping Skill #5

1. What skill did you choose?

2. Why do you think this skill might work for you?

3. When could you use it in your life?

4. How would using this skill make your life different?

5. What might get in the way of using it—and how can you plan around that?

Coping Skill #6

1. What skill did you choose?

2. Why do you think this skill might work for you?

3. When could you use it in your life?

4. How would using this skill make your life different?

5. What might get in the way of using it—and how can you plan around that?

Coping Skill #7

1. What skill did you choose?

2. Why do you think this skill might work for you?

3. When could you use it in your life?

4. How would using this skill make your life different?

5. What might get in the way of using it—and how can you plan around that?

Coping Skill #8

1. What skill did you choose?

2. Why do you think this skill might work for you?

3. When could you use it in your life?

4. How would using this skill make your life different?

5. What might get in the way of using it—and how can you plan around that?

Coping Skill #9

1. What skill did you choose?

2. Why do you think this skill might work for you?

3. When could you use it in your life?

4. How would using this skill make your life different?

5. What might get in the way of using it—and how can you plan around that?

Coping Skill #10

1. What skill did you choose?

2. Why do you think this skill might work for you?

3. When could you use it in your life?

4. How would using this skill make your life different?

5. What might get in the way of using it—and how can you plan around that?

Building a Tactile Coping Skills Toolbox

Group TWO: Worksheet Two

Building a Tactile Coping Skills Toolbox

This worksheet will guide you in creating a personal coping skills toolbox—something you can carry with you when you know stress, triggers, or emotional overwhelm might show up. This toolbox can help you manage emotions, stay grounded, and feel more in control in your recovery journey.

What is a Tactile Coping Skills Toolbox?

A tactile coping skills toolbox is a collection of small, sensory-focused items that you can use when you're feeling overwhelmed, anxious, frustrated, or disconnected. These tools help ground you in the present moment and reduce distress. It's especially useful for adults who want something practical, discreet, and transportable.

Step 1: Choosing the Right Container
• Use something you already own—like a backpack, purse, fanny pack, makeup bag, or lunchbox.
  • Pick something that won't draw attention, so it doesn't feel awkward or obvious.
  • Make sure it's easy to carry and open, and has enough compartments or pockets.

Step 2: What to Include in Your Toolbox
Include a mix of items that appeal to different senses (touch, smell, sight, hearing). Try to pick tools that help you calm down, refocus, or self-soothe.
  • Stress ball or therapy putty
  • Fidget toy (spinner, cube, stretchy band)
  • Smooth stone or worry stone
  • Scented lotion or essential oil roller
  • Small notebook and pen for jotting thoughts

• Affirmation cards or quote cards
• Earbuds and a calming music playlist
• Peppermint gum or sour candy (for taste/sensation)
• A printed grounding technique or breathing card
• A photo of someone or something that gives you strength
• Mindfulness cards or small coloring book and pencils

Step 3: When to Bring and Use Your Toolbox
Bring your toolbox with you to places or situations where you might feel:
• Emotionally vulnerable or overstimulated
• Triggered or anxious
• In conflict with someone
• Overwhelmed in public settings or on transit
• Going to therapy, recovery meetings, or medical appointments
• At work or school during high-stress moments
• Having conversations where you struggle with boundaries

Step 4: How to Use the Tools
Use one or more items when you notice signs of stress or dysregulation:
• Tight chest or shallow breathing? Try your breathing card or essential oil.
• Racing thoughts? Use the journal or affirmation cards.
• Restlessness? Use a fidget toy, stress ball, or chew gum.
Practice using these tools even when you feel okay, so it's easier to reach for them when you need them
.

Reflection: My Toolbox Plan
1. What type of bag or container will I use for my toolbox?

2. List five items I want to include and why:

3. Where do I plan to keep my toolbox?

4. What situations do I know I'll want to bring it with me to?

5. How will I remind myself to use it when I need it?

Group Three: Triggers and Cravings Management

Group Three: Triggers and Cravings Management

Summary: Explore personal triggers and how to handle cravings effectively.

Objectives:
- Identify personal triggers.
- Develop strategies to manage cravings.

References: "The Craving Mind" by Judson Brewer.
Supplemental Reading: "Get Your Loved One Sober" by Meyers & Wolfe.

How to Facilitate:

- Discuss common triggers and cravings.
- Use a brainstorming session to identify client-specific triggers.

Activities:

• Have clients complete a triggers worksheet. Pair clients for role-playing strategies.

Clinician's Notes: Group Three

Clinician's Notes: Group Three

Clinician's Preparation & Core Knowledge

Group Three focuses on understanding and managing triggers and cravings—core components of relapse prevention. This session helps clients identify internal (emotions, thoughts) and external (people, places, situations) triggers, and develop practical strategies to respond differently.

Review Judson Brewer's neuroscience-based framework in 'The Craving Mind,' which explains how habit loops form through trigger–behavior–reward cycles. Be prepared to explain how cravings are not just about willpower—they are conditioned responses that can be disrupted through awareness and mindfulness.

Understand the importance of de-shaming the experience of cravings. Your goal is to move clients from fear and suppression to curiosity and skillful response.

Essential Talking Points for Clients

- "Cravings aren't emergencies—they're invitations to respond differently."
- "Triggers can't always be avoided, but they can be anticipated and prepared for."
- "The more you observe your cravings without acting on them, the more power you reclaim."
- "You are not your craving. You are the person who gets to decide what to do next."

Engagement Tips to Make This Group Come Alive

- Use a whiteboard or flip chart to visually map out the 'Trigger → Craving → Response → Outcome' sequence.
- Invite clients to share surprising or subtle triggers they've noticed (e.g., music, smells, routines). This normalizes and expands awareness.

- Use a craving scale (0–10) and have clients reflect on where cravings land for them, and how intensity shifts over time.

- Introduce mindfulness as a tool to ride the craving wave. Consider leading a 2-minute 'urge surfing' exercise.

- Pair clients to role-play common trigger scenarios and practice applying alternate responses (calling a support person, grounding skill, changing environment).

- Challenge the group to brainstorm coping strategies by category: physical, emotional, cognitive, social, and spiritual.

Final Word to the Clinician

This week is about transforming unconscious reactions into conscious choices. Help clients deconstruct the craving cycle and replace shame with curiosity and skill-building. Avoid lecturing—use collaborative discovery and normalizing language to keep the group engaged. By the end of this session, participants should feel more empowered to anticipate, understand, and manage the urges that once felt unmanageable.

Triggers

Group THREE: Worksheet One

Triggers

Understanding your personal triggers is a critical part of managing cravings and staying on track with your recovery goals. This worksheet is designed to help you identify the people, places, feelings, and situations that trigger urges to use, and to start building awareness of how to respond differently.

Step 1: Identify Your Triggers

Think about the last few times you had strong cravings or used. What led up to it? List your triggers below:

• People who trigger me:

• Places that are triggering:

• Times of day or routines that feel triggering:

• Emotions that lead to cravings (e.g., anger, loneliness):

• Physical states (e.g., tired, hungry, in pain):

• Events or anniversaries that bring up memories:

• Thoughts or beliefs that trigger me:

• Other environmental or situational triggers:

Step 2: Trigger Response Mapping

Pick one of the triggers you listed above and answer the following questions:

1. What is the trigger?

2. What usually happens when you're triggered in this way?

3. What thoughts or beliefs come up in your mind when this happens?

4. What do you usually do next?

5. What would you *like* to do differently in the future?

6. What could help you respond in that new way? (e.g., skill, tool, person, environment)

Step 3: Plan Ahead

Think about a high-risk situation that could happen this week. Use the prompts below to plan ahead.

1. What is a situation you expect could be triggering?

2. What are 2–3 coping strategies you could use if the trigger arises?

3. Who can you reach out to for support?

4. What can you do *before* this situation to set yourself up for success?

5. What will you do *after* the situation to care for yourself and reflect?

Remember: Triggers are not failures—they're opportunities for awareness and growth. The more you notice them, the more power you have to choose a different response.

Cravings Scale

Group THREE: Worksheet Two

Cravings Scale

Cravings are a natural part of recovery. This worksheet will help you reflect on your recent cravings, understand their intensity, and build a strategy for responding to them in a healthy, empowered way. Use this tool as often as needed to track your cravings and increase your ability to ride them out.

Step 1: The Craving Scale (0–10)

Use this scale to rate your craving intensity. Zero means no craving at all, and ten means an overwhelming craving you feel unable to resist.

0 – No craving at all

1–3 – Mild craving; I notice it, but it's easy to ignore or distract from

4–6 – Moderate craving; I feel it strongly and need to use skills to manage it

7–8 – Strong craving; very distracting and hard to shake

9–10 – Intense craving; feels overwhelming, like I might act on it without support or intervention

Step 2: Reflect on a Recent Craving

Think about a craving you experienced recently. Answer the questions below.

1. What triggered this craving? (e.g., place, person, feeling, memory)

2. On a scale of 0–10, how strong was the craving?

3. What thoughts went through your mind during the craving?

4. What did you do in response?

5. Did anything help lessen the craving?

6. Looking back, would you respond differently next time?

Step 3: Create a Craving Response Plan

Use this space to write strategies that help you based on the intensity of your cravings. Choose specific actions that help you stay grounded and avoid acting on urges.

Low (1–3) Craving:
Recommended strategies: Distraction (music, walking, journaling), deep breathing, talking to a friend

Moderate (4–6) Craving:
Recommended strategies: Grounding exercises, mindfulness, reviewing reasons for recovery, using a coping tool

High (7–10) Craving:
Recommended strategies: Remove self from triggering environment, call a support person, use crisis plan, go to a meeting, ride out the craving with focused breathing and self-talk

Step 4: Remind Yourself

Write yourself a reminder for when cravings feel overwhelming. Use your own words to affirm your strength.
Example: "Cravings are temporary. I've gotten through them before, and I can do it again."
My Personal Reminder

Group Four: Building Relationships

Group Four: Building Relationships

Summary: Examine how substance use impacts relationships and develop improved dynamics.

Objectives:

- Recognize relationship patterns that no longer feel helpful.
- Learn effective communication techniques.

References: "Attached: The New Science of Adult Attachment" by Amir Levine & Rachel Heller.
Supplemental Reading: "The Seven Principles for Making Marriage Work" by John Gottman.

How to Facilitate:

- Use a lecture-discussion format.
- Introduce key concepts of relationships.

Activities:

- Conduct a role-play to practice communication.
- Have clients journal about their current relationships.

C linician's Notes: Group Four

Clinician's Preparation & Core Knowledge

Group Four invites clients to reflect on the way substance use has influenced their connections with others, and how to move toward more supportive, fulfilling relationships. Rather than framing relationships as simply 'healthy' or 'toxic,' this session focuses on helping clients evaluate which relationships improve their quality of life and align with their values.

Prepare by reviewing key ideas from attachment theory (Levine & Heller) and the research-backed communication strategies of John Gottman. Understanding how attachment styles (anxious, avoidant, secure) affect relationship behaviors will help you guide clients in identifying patterns without judgment.

Frame boundaries as tools for self-differentiation—not as walls or punishments. Boundaries allow individuals to communicate needs, protect emotional safety, and navigate relationships with clarity and self-respect.

Essential Talking Points for Clients

- "Substance use often changes how we show up in relationships—and how others show up for us."
- "Supportive relationships feel mutual, safe, and aligned with your values."
- "Boundaries are not about pushing people away—they're about expressing what matters to you and protecting your well-being."
- "Learning how to communicate clearly helps reduce conflict and deepen connection."

Engagement Tips to Make This Group Come Alive

- Begin with a discussion: What makes a relationship feel supportive versus draining? Let clients define their own markers.

- Present attachment styles with simple examples (e.g., anxious: fears abandonment, avoidant: needs space, secure: balances closeness and independence).

- Use a relationship mapping exercise: Who do I turn to when I need support? Who feels aligned with who I'm becoming?

- Facilitate a communication role-play: One client expresses a boundary or need, the other practices listening and reflective feedback.

- Introduce 'I' statements and reflective listening as tools, not rules—emphasize authenticity over perfection.

- Normalize that rebuilding or repairing relationships takes time, and that not all relationships can or should be restored.

Final Word to the Clinician

This session can stir up grief, hope, and discomfort. Meet clients where they are—some may be re-establishing relationships, while others are grieving disconnection. Emphasize that relationship repair is a journey, and each client has the right to build a support system that honors their growth and well-being. Focus on helping them articulate their needs, recognize their values, and connect with people who respect both.

Reflecting on Relationships in Recovery

Group FOUR: Worksheet One

Reflecting on Relationships in Recovery

Recovery often brings major shifts in relationships. Some relationships help us grow and stay on track with our goals. Others may feel less aligned with the life we're building. This worksheet helps you reflect on the relationships you're closest to, evaluate how they support or hinder your recovery, and consider changes you may want to make.

Step 1: Who Are Your Closest Relationships?

List the 3–5 people you feel most connected to right now. These could be friends, family members, romantic partners, coworkers, etc.

1.
2.
3.
4.
5.

Step 2: What Helps?

Circle any of the following qualities that apply to your relationships and support your recovery and well-being:

- They respect my boundaries
- They listen without judgment
- They encourage my sobriety
- They help me feel safe
- They support my goals
- We can talk about difficult things
- They show up when I need them
- They model healthy coping skills
- We laugh and enjoy time together

Write about one relationship that supports your recovery and why:

Step 3: What Might Be Holding You Back?

Circle any of the following behaviors or patterns that feel harmful or discouraging in your relationships:
- They pressure me to use substances
- They ignore or cross my boundaries
- I feel judged or criticized
- They bring chaos or drama into my life
- They don't support my recovery
- I feel I have to hide my truth around them
- They expect more from me than I can give
- I leave interactions feeling drained or anxious

Write about one relationship that feels hard or complicated right now, and what makes it feel that way:

Step 4: Clarifying Next Steps

Now that you've reflected on how your relationships are affecting you, answer the following questions to clarify your next steps:

1. Which relationships feel most aligned with your goals and values?

2. Which ones might need clearer boundaries, space, or change?

3. What's one small thing you can do this week to improve or protect a relationship that matters to you?

Remember: Recovery is not just about changing your relationship to substances—it's also about changing your relationship with people, boundaries, and yourself. You deserve connection that uplifts, not connection that depletes.

Understanding Your Attachment Style

Group FOUR: Worksheet Two

Understanding Your Attachment Style

Attachment styles are patterns we develop early in life that shape how we connect with others. In recovery, understanding your attachment style can help you build stronger, more supportive relationships. This worksheet will guide you through identifying your likely attachment style and exploring how it may influence your recovery journey.

Step 1: What Are Attachment Styles?

There are four main types of attachment styles:

Secure – You feel comfortable with closeness and trust in relationships. You can rely on others and let them rely on you.

Anxious – You may fear abandonment, crave closeness, and worry about others pulling away.

Avoidant – You value independence and may feel uncomfortable with emotional closeness or vulnerability.

Fearful (Disorganized) – You may want closeness but also fear it, often feeling conflicted or unsure.

Step 2: Self-Assessment

Reflect on your experiences and check the statements that feel true for you:

Secure Attachment Indicators:

◈ I'm generally comfortable depending on others and having others depend on me.

◈ I trust others and feel confident in close relationships.

◈ I can ask for help when I need it.

Anxious Attachment Indicators:

◈ I often worry that people I care about will leave me.

◈ I need frequent reassurance in relationships.

◈ I tend to feel 'too much' or 'not enough' for others.

Avoidant Attachment Indicators:

◈ I feel uncomfortable relying on others.

◈ I struggle to express my feelings or let people get close.

◈ I value independence and prefer to solve problems alone.

Fearful Attachment Indicators:

◈ I want closeness, but I also fear being hurt.

◈ I find relationships confusing or emotionally overwhelming.

◈ I sometimes push people away even when I want connection.

Step 3: Reflection

Which attachment style do you think most fits you based on the checked items? Why?

How has this attachment style shown up in past relationships?

How might this style impact your ability to build supportive relationships in recovery?

Step 4: Moving Forward

Here are a few ideas for working with your attachment style in recovery:

• If you identify as **anxious**, practice self-reassurance and build relationships with consistent, trustworthy people.

• If you identify as **avoidant**, take small steps to express needs and allow closeness.

• If you identify as **fearful**, work with a therapist to process early attachment wounds and build safe connection habits.

• If you identify as **secure**, lean into your strengths and be a model of healthy connection for others.

Attachment styles aren't fixed. With awareness, support, and practice, you can move toward more secure ways of connecting with others.

Group Five: Relapse Prevention Planning

G roup Five: Relapse Prevention Planning

Summary: Focus on strategies to prevent relapse and maintain recovery.

Objectives:
- Identify high-risk situations.
-Develop a personalized relapse prevention plan.

References: "Staying Sober: A Guide for Relapse Prevention" by Terence T. Gorski.
Supplemental Reading: "Mindfulness-Based Relapse Prevention for Addictive Behaviors" by Bowen et al.

How to Facilitate:

- Explain the importance of relapse prevention.
- Provide examples of effective plans.

Activities:

- Guide clients through a worksheet to create their plan.
- Facilitate a group discussion on challenges.

Clinician's Notes: Group Five

Clinician's Notes: GroupFive

Clinician's Preparation & Core Knowledge

Group Five is designed to help clients proactively plan for the inevitable challenges of recovery by developing a personalized relapse prevention strategy. Grounded in Terence Gorski's model and supported by mindfulness-based relapse prevention research, this session shifts the focus from fear of relapse to empowerment through preparation.

Review common high-risk situations, such as HALT (Hungry, Angry, Lonely, Tired), anniversaries, or conflict, and discuss cognitive, emotional, and situational cues that can trigger relapse. Integrate mindfulness as a tool for becoming aware of urges without acting on them.

Approach relapse planning as a compassionate process—not about anticipating a lapse, but about building resilience and reducing shame. The more clients understand their unique risk points, the more confidently they can manage them.

Essential Talking Points for Clients

- "Relapse doesn't start with the drink or drug—it starts with disconnection from your recovery tools."
- "Relapse prevention is not about expecting to lapse. It's about knowing how to protect your progress."
- "Everyone has different high-risk moments. Knowing yours helps you stay one step ahead."
- "A relapse prevention plan is a living document—you can adapt it as your life and needs change."

Engagement Tips to Make This Group Come Alive

- Begin with a story illustrating how a relapse unfolded over time—highlight subtle warning signs.

- Use a visual timeline or worksheet to map out early warning signs, triggering thoughts, and effective responses.

- Normalize struggle. Invite clients to reflect on past relapses (if any) without shame, focusing on what they learned.

- Present real-life scenarios (e.g., a stressful family dinner, payday, isolation) and ask the group how they'd handle them.

- Introduce the concept of a 'recovery action plan'—who to call, where to go, what to do if cravings spike.

- Facilitate brainstorming on practical skills: distraction, grounding, calling a peer, or using a mantra or affirmation.

Final Word to the Clinician

This session is where insight meets action. Help clients feel proud—not anxious—about crafting a plan that reflects self-awareness and care. Emphasize that setbacks can be learning moments, not endpoints. When clients leave this session, they should feel like they're walking away with a map—and a toolkit—to help them navigate what's ahead.

22

Relapse / Recurrence of Use Prevention Plan

WEEK FIVE: Worksheet One

Relapse / Recurrence of Use Prevention Plan

This plan is designed to help you stay grounded, self-aware, and connected to your recovery path. Use it as a tool to reflect on your strengths, identify warning signs, and prepare for moments of challenge.

Section 1: My Cycle of Addiction

Reflect on what your personal cycle of addiction looks like. Include triggers, use patterns, consequences, and feelings.

My personal addiction cycle:

Section 2: Triggers and Cravings

List the people, places, thoughts, or emotions that typically trigger cravings:

How do cravings feel in your body and mind? What has helped you ride them out in the past?

Section 3: Early Warning Signs

What signs do you notice that might indicate you're moving toward use?
• Skipping meetings or therapy
• Isolating from support
• Justifying 'just one use'

• Increased stress, shame, or emotional reactivity
• Glamorizing past use
Other personal warning signs:

Section 4: Coping Skills Toolbox

List the coping skills that work best for you when you're triggered or overwhelmed:

Section 5: Boundaries

What boundaries do you need to maintain your recovery? Think about time, space, energy, and people.

Section 6: Safe People & Safe Places

List the people you can call or reach out to when you're struggling:
1.
2.
3.

Safe places you can go if you need support or distance from a trigger:
1.
2.
3.

Section 7: Crisis Plan

What will you do if you are in immediate danger of using? Who will you contact? Where will you go?

Section 8: Letter to My Future Self

Write a letter to yourself from the version of you that is calm, grounded, and committed to recovery. This is for the version of you that might be struggling and thinking about returning to use.

Dear Me,

Love,
Me

Section 9: Accountability

Who helps hold you accountable to your recovery goals? What does that look like?

Section 10: Commitments

List a few specific commitments to yourself that will help you stay on track. Examples:
• I will attend at least one support group each week
• I will reach out when I'm struggling
• I will keep my coping skills toolbox stocked and nearby

My own recovery commitments:

Group Six: Mindfulness and Meditation

Group Six: Mindfulness and Meditation

Summary: Introduce mindfulness practices to reduce stress and increase awareness.

Objectives:
- Understand the benefits of mindfulness.
- Practice basic meditation techniques.

References: "Wherever You Go, There You Are" by Jon Kabat-Zinn.
Supplemental Reading: "The Mindful Path to Addiction Recovery" by Lawrence Peltz.

How to Facilitate:
- Begin with an explanation of mindfulness.
- Lead a short guided meditation.

Activities:
- Practice a mindfulness exercise such as mindful breathing.
- Reflect on the experience in a group discussion.

Clinician's Notes: Group Six

Clinician's Notes: Group Six

Clinician's Preparation & Core Knowledge

Group Six introduces clients to mindfulness and meditation as accessible, nonjudgmental tools for increasing self-awareness and reducing emotional reactivity. Drawing from Jon Kabat-Zinn's foundational work and supported by addiction-specific applications from Lawrence Peltz, this session empowers clients to pause, notice, and respond instead of react.

Prepare by understanding the core principles of mindfulness: presence, nonjudgment, and curiosity. Practice a short guided meditation yourself before the session so you can lead it with calm and confidence. Clients do not need to clear their minds—help them focus on *noticing* thoughts and sensations without attaching to them.

Normalize restlessness, discomfort, or resistance. Many clients have trauma histories, so be prepared to offer grounding alternatives (eyes open, feet movement, brief duration) and always make participation voluntary.

Essential Talking Points for Clients

- "Mindfulness isn't about emptying your mind. It's about paying attention, on purpose, to the present moment."
- "When you slow down and notice what's happening inside you, you create space to choose how you respond."
- "You don't have to do this perfectly—every time you notice your mind has wandered and bring it back, that's the practice."
- "Mindfulness can help you stay grounded when cravings or emotions try to take over."

Engagement Tips to Make This Group Come Alive

- Begin by asking the group: What do you think of when you hear the word 'mindfulness'? Clarify myths and preconceptions.

- Offer different formats: breathing, sensory awareness, body scan, or mindful listening. Let clients choose what feels accessible.

- Start small—a 2-minute guided breathing exercise with eyes open can be less intimidating than a full meditation.

- Create a low-pressure atmosphere. Let clients know it's normal to feel distracted or fidgety.

- Use analogies: mindfulness is like watching clouds pass in the sky, or observing traffic without jumping into the road.

- End with a reflection prompt: What did you notice? Was anything surprising or uncomfortable? How might this be useful in recovery?

Final Word to the Clinician

This week is about planting a seed. Mindfulness won't feel transformative to everyone immediately, but your goal is to offer a practice they can return to when life gets loud. Keep it simple, invitational, and compassionate. Emphasize that even one mindful breath in a stressful moment is a success. You're offering a lifelong tool that clients can grow into over time.

25

Mindfulness Meditation & Reflection

Group SIX: Worksheet One

Mindfulness Meditation & Reflection

Mindfulness is the practice of paying attention, on purpose, in the present moment, without judgment. This worksheet includes a guided mindfulness meditation that your clinician can read aloud, followed by reflection questions to help deepen your experience.

Guided Meditation: Grounding in the Present Moment

Find a comfortable seated position. Allow your hands to rest gently in your lap or by your sides. If you feel safe, gently close your eyes or soften your gaze.

Begin by taking a slow, deep breath in through your nose... and let it out slowly through your mouth. Again, inhale... and exhale. Let your body settle into stillness.

Bring your attention to your feet. Feel the ground beneath you — the pressure, the contact, the stability. Now bring your attention to your seat. Feel the support of the chair or cushion beneath you.

Gently bring your awareness to your breath. You don't need to change it — just notice it. The rise and fall. The in and out. If your mind wanders, that's okay. Just notice where it went and kindly bring it back to your breath.

Now, silently say to yourself: 'In this moment, I am safe. I am breathing. I am here.' Repeat this quietly in your mind with each breath for the next few moments.

As you near the end of this meditation, begin to bring awareness back to your surroundings. Wiggle your fingers and toes. Notice any sounds in the room. And when you're ready, gently open your eyes.

Reflection Questions

Take a few moments to reflect on your experience and write your thoughts below.

1. What did you notice during the meditation?

2. How did your body feel before, during, and after the practice?

3. Were there any thoughts or emotions that stood out?

4. Did your mind wander? If so, how did it feel to bring it back?

5. How might you use this practice in your day-to-day life?

6. What environment or time of day feels best for you to practice mindfulness?

7. What words or affirmations felt most grounding for you?

Mindfulness is a skill that grows with practice. You can return to this meditation whenever you feel overwhelmed, disconnected, or in need of grounding. Over time, it can become a powerful tool in your recovery journey.

26

Group Seven: Emotional Regulation

Group Seven: Emotional Regulation

Summary: Teach clients how to identify and manage their emotions effectively.

Objectives:
- Recognize emotional triggers.
- Learn strategies to regulate intense emotions.

References: "DBT Skills Training Manual" by Marsha Linehan.
Supplemental Reading: "Emotional Intelligence 2.0" by Travis Bradberry and Jean Greaves.

How to Facilitate:
- Discuss common emotional regulation challenges.
- Provide examples of regulation techniques.

Activities:

- Practice deep breathing exercises.
- Use emotion regulation worksheet to identify triggers and responses.

Note: This session draws from Dialectical Behavior Therapy (DBT), developed by Marsha Linehan. For full materials and skills training handouts, see Linehan, M. (2015). DBT Skills Training Manual (2nd ed.).

C linician's Notes: Group Seven

Clinician's Preparation & Core Knowledge

Group Seven focuses on helping clients identify, understand, and regulate intense emotions—skills that are vital for recovery and relapse prevention. This session draws from Dialectical Behavior Therapy (DBT) and emotional intelligence research, emphasizing that emotions are not the problem—unmanaged emotional responses are what often lead to difficulty.

Familiarize yourself with DBT-informed strategies such as deep breathing, opposite action, and 'checking the facts.' These techniques help clients respond to emotional distress in a more grounded way. Emotional Intelligence frameworks also emphasize self-awareness, emotional labeling, and impulse control—valuable skills for those navigating early recovery.

Create a nonjudgmental space where clients can explore their emotional lives. Many may carry shame about being 'too emotional' or about numbing for years. Affirm that learning to feel and regulate is not only possible—it's a core part of healing.

Essential Talking Points for Clients

- "Emotions are data, not directives. You don't have to act on every feeling—but you can learn from them."
- "Emotional regulation doesn't mean not feeling. It means giving yourself choices when you do feel."
- "Learning to name your emotions helps you manage them—'name it to tame it.'"
- "The goal isn't perfection, it's progress. Every time you pause before reacting, you're building emotional strength."

Engagement Tips to Make This Group Come Alive

- Start with a check-in using an emotion wheel. Ask: 'What are you feeling right now?' and normalize multiple or mixed feelings.

- Use real-world examples of dysregulated emotions (e.g., snapping at a partner, impulsive spending) and ask the group: What could have helped?

- Lead a guided deep breathing or 4-7-8 breathing technique and debrief how it felt.

- Demonstrate 'checking the facts' or 'opposite action' using a fictional but relatable client scenario.

- Distribute or walk through an emotion regulation worksheet. Ask: What triggered this emotion? What was my initial response? What else could I try?

- Encourage clients to keep a simple mood journal during the week—rate mood, identify triggers, and note what helped.

Final Word to the Clinician

Emotional regulation is not intuitive for many people, especially those who've used substances to cope. Your role this week is to normalize emotional ups and downs, offer hope that change is possible, and provide small, manageable tools for navigating difficult feelings. If even one client leaves knowing they have a choice between reacting and pausing—they've taken a meaningful step toward long-term recovery.

28

Emotion Regulation

Group Seven: Worksheet One

Emotion Regulation

Understanding your emotional landscape is essential for maintaining recovery. This worksheet will guide you in identifying your emotional triggers, recognizing your responses, and building strategies to support your emotional well-being.

Everyone has different emotional triggers, and that's okay. Your experiences, history, and environment shape how emotions show up for you. This worksheet includes common and complex emotions to help you reflect on your unique emotional patterns.

Section 1: Common Emotions and Sample Triggers

Use this list to help identify what emotions you've experienced recently.

Anger: e.g., Being ignored, feeling disrespected, unmet expectations

Sadness: e.g., Loss, loneliness, change, unresolved grief

Fear: e.g., Uncertainty, past trauma, conflict, health issues

Guilt: e.g., Breaking personal values, hurting others, past actions

Shame: e.g., Feeling inadequate, judged, or unworthy

Joy: e.g., Connection, success, feeling understood

Gratitude: e.g., Appreciating small things, acts of kindness

Jealousy: e.g., Comparison, perceived unfairness, fear of losing something

Relief: e.g., Resolution of stress, support received

Embarrassment: e.g., Public mistakes, social discomfort

Love: e.g., Feeling valued, deep connection, care

Pride: e.g., Personal achievement, recognition, self-improvement

Section 2: Emotional Awareness

List 3 emotions you experience frequently and describe what typically triggers them.
1. Emotion: _____ | Trigger: _____

2. Emotion: _____ | Trigger: _____

3. Emotion: _____ | Trigger: _____

Section 3: Emotional Responses

For each emotion above, describe how you usually respond and how it impacts your recovery.
Example: 'When I feel anxious, I isolate and skip meetings, which makes me feel worse.'

Section 4: Positive Emotions and Recovery

Positive emotions can help strengthen your recovery by reinforcing healthy behaviors and self-worth.
List some emotions that support your recovery and strategies to cultivate them:
Emotion: _____ | How it supports me: _____

Strategy to increase this emotion: _____

Repeat for more: _____

Section 5: Challenging Emotions

Identify emotions that are difficult to manage and might threaten your recovery.
Emotion: _____ | What it makes me want to do: _____

How can I ride it out or respond in a healthy way?

Section 6: Distress Tolerance Skills

List at least 3 skills you can use when a strong emotion arises:
1. Grounding exercise or mindful breathing
2. Calling a supportive person
3. Doing something creative or distracting (e.g., drawing, music, walking)
Your own ideas:

Section 7: Reflection

How has understanding your emotional patterns helped your recovery so far?

What is one thing you want to do differently the next time you feel overwhelmed?

Group Eight: Self-Esteem Building

G roup Eight: Self-Esteem Building

Summary: Explore the importance of self-esteem in recovery and learn ways to build it.

Objectives:
- Understand the role of self-esteem in recovery.
- Develop strategies to improve self-esteem.

References: "The Self-Esteem Workbook" by Glenn Schiraldi.
Supplemental Reading: "You Can Heal Your Life" by Louise Hay.

How to Facilitate:
- Introduce the concept of self-esteem and its impact on recovery.
- Facilitate a discussion on personal strengths.

Activities:
- Create a strengths-based affirmation list.
- Reflect on achievements and positive attributes through journaling.

Clinician's Notes: Group Eight

Clinician's Notes: Group Eight

Clinician's Preparation & Core Knowledge

Group Eight focuses on the concept of self-esteem—how individuals view their own worth—and how strengthening it can reinforce recovery. Many clients come into treatment with damaged self-concept due to years of stigma, internalized shame, or unresolved trauma. Helping them reconnect with a sense of value and possibility is both healing and practical.

Prepare by reviewing material from Glenn Schiraldi's cognitive-behavioral approach to self-esteem and Louise Hay's emphasis on affirmation and self-compassion. These two resources offer both structured and reflective pathways for reclaiming a more positive relationship with the self.

Focus on strength-based facilitation. This is not a time to dissect what's 'wrong' with the client. Instead, emphasize their resilience, creativity, and capacity to grow—even in pain.

Essential Talking Points for Clients

- "Self-esteem isn't about thinking you're perfect—it's about believing you're worthy of love and growth."
- "Low self-esteem can make recovery harder. But recovery also creates space to rebuild how you see yourself."
- "You've already survived so much—let's start noticing the strengths that helped you get here."
- "When you talk to yourself, would you say those words to a friend? If not, it's time to practice new ones."

Engagement Tips to Make This Group Come Alive

- Begin by asking: 'What do you think self-esteem means?' Validate a range of definitions and emotional reactions.

- Introduce affirmations as intentional self-messages, not magical thinking. Allow space for skepticism or discomfort.

- Have clients list 3 personal strengths and turn them into affirmations (e.g., 'I am resourceful' or 'I am still learning, and that's okay').

- Provide prompts for journaling: 'One thing I've survived is...' or 'A time I surprised myself was...'

- Encourage group members to write an affirmation or kind message to another (optional and anonymous).

- Close by reflecting on how positive self-talk or inner encouragement can shape recovery efforts.

Final Word to the Clinician

This session can feel vulnerable—self-esteem touches old wounds. Let the tone be gentle, curious, and empowering. Your presence matters more than perfection here. Simply by creating a space where clients are reminded of their worth, you're offering a recovery tool they can return to long after treatment ends.

31

Strength-Based Affirmations and Discovery

Group EIGHT: Worksheet One

Strength-Based Affirmations and Discovery

Part 1: Strength-Based Affirmations

These affirmations are designed to help you focus on your strengths, resilience, and recovery journey. You can repeat them daily, write them in a journal, or choose a few that resonate with you the most.

- I am stronger than my cravings.
- I have overcome difficult things before, and I can do it again.
- I am learning and growing every day.
- My past does not define me—my choices today do.
- I am worthy of love, healing, and peace.
- I trust myself to take the next right step.
- Each moment is a new opportunity to choose recovery.
- I am building a life I am proud of.
- I am not alone; I have support.
- I honor the progress I've made, no matter how small it may seem.

Part 2: Discovering Your Strengths

Use these reflective questions to help identify your inner strengths. There is no right or wrong answer—be honest, kind, and curious about yourself.

1. What is one challenge I have overcome that I'm proud of? What did I do to get through it?

2. What are some things others have complimented me on in the past?

3. When do I feel the most confident or capable? What am I doing in those moments?

4. What personal values are important to me? How do I live them out?

5. Who do I admire, and what qualities do I see in them that I also have?

6. What have I learned from my recovery journey so far? What strengths has it revealed in me?

7. How do I support others in my life? What does that say about my character?

8. What motivates me to keep moving forward?

9. What does resilience mean to me, and how have I shown it?

10. How do I want to use my strengths to build the life I want?

Part 3: Acknowledging and Affirming Your Strengths

Now, complete the following sentences in your own words:

One of my strengths is _____.

I've shown this strength when _____.

This strength helps me in my recovery by _____.

Another strength I am beginning to recognize in myself is _____.

I can remind myself of these strengths when I feel _____.

Group Nine: Financial Management in Recovery

G roup Nine: Financial Management in Recovery

Summary: Teach clients the basics of financial management and budgeting.

Objectives:

- Understand the importance of financial stability in recovery.
- Learn basic budgeting techniques.

References: "Your Money or Your Life" by Vicki Robin.
Supplemental Reading: "Total Money Makeover" by Dave Ramsey.

How to Facilitate:
- Discuss the role of financial stress in relapse.
- Teach basic budgeting and saving strategies.

Activities:
- Have clients create a mock budget.
- Role-play scenarios involving financial decisions.

Clinician's Notes: Group Nine

C linician's Notes: Group Nine

Clinician's Preparation & Core Knowledge

Group Nine helps clients connect the dots between financial stress and substance use, while offering practical tools to promote financial empowerment. Many people in recovery have histories of unstable income, impulsive spending, or debt accumulation tied to survival or addiction. This session emphasizes dignity, not judgment, while providing a clear framework for rebuilding financial habits.

Familiarize yourself with accessible budgeting concepts like needs vs. wants, tracking expenses, and creating a simple spending plan. Draw from Vicki Robin's values-based approach to money, and Dave Ramsey's debt-reduction and savings strategies—while avoiding any shame-based tone.

Approach this week with patience. Financial topics often bring up anxiety, shame, or avoidance. Your goal is to help clients take one manageable step toward clarity and control.

Essential Talking Points for Clients

- "Financial stress is one of the top triggers for relapse—and one of the most common barriers to recovery stability."
- "Budgeting isn't about restriction—it's about clarity and choice."
- "You don't have to be perfect with money to feel more confident about it. Small steps add up."
- "It's okay if you've made money mistakes in the past. What matters is what you do next."

Engagement Tips to Make This Group Come Alive

- Start with a discussion: 'What were you taught—or not taught—about money growing up?' This builds empathy and insight.

- Use a mock budget worksheet with example categories: rent, food, phone, debt, fun. Let clients customize it for their real or future life.

- Avoid judgmental language. Emphasize values-based spending and harm reduction (e.g., building toward better choices, not perfection).

- Role-play scenarios: e.g., managing an unexpected expense, saying no to lending money, or prioritizing bills when funds are limited.

- Introduce the idea of an 'emergency fund' or 'sobriety savings goal' as practical and empowering.

- Offer free or low-cost financial planning resources, if available locally or online (e.g., extension services, nonprofit tools).

Final Word to the Clinician

Financial repair takes time, and for many clients, this may be the first time they've had a conversation about money that isn't filled with judgment. Be warm, clear, and encouraging. Your role is to spark momentum—to remind clients that building a stable future includes building a plan for their money, one choice at a time.

34

Mock Budget

Group NINE: Worksheet One

Mock Budget

This worksheet is designed to help you build a monthly budget, track your spending, and evaluate your financial needs and goals. You can fill this out to see where your money goes and plan how to use your income wisely.

Section 1: Monthly Income

List all sources of monthly income (after taxes):
Primary job: $_____
Secondary job: $_____
Government assistance: $_____
Child support/alimony: $_____
Other (specify): $_____
TOTAL MONTHLY INCOME: $_____

Section 2: Monthly Expenses

List your estimated monthly expenses below:
Rent/Mortgage: $_____
Utilities (electric, water, gas): $_____
Phone/Internet: $_____
Groceries: $_____
Transportation (gas, bus fare, car insurance): $_____
Health care/Medications: $_____
Child care: $_____
Debt payments (credit cards, loans): $_____
Entertainment: $_____
Personal care (hygiene, haircuts, etc.): $_____

Savings: $_____
Other (specify): $_____
TOTAL MONTHLY EXPENSES: $_____

Section 3: Budget Summary

Use this section to calculate and reflect on your financial status.
Total Monthly Income: $_____
Minus Total Monthly Expenses: $_____
Leftover / Overdrawn Amount: $_____
Do I need to reduce any expenses? _____
What can I do to increase income or savings? _____
My next financial goal is: _____

Section 4: Reflection

Answer the following questions to reflect on your financial habits and goals.
1. What spending categories are most important to me?

2. Where do I notice I might overspend or struggle to stay within a budget?

3. What small change could I make this month to improve my budget?

4. How does financial stress impact my recovery, and how can budgeting help reduce that stress?

35

Financial Reflection

Group NINE: Worksheet Two

Financial Reflection

This worksheet is designed to help you reflect on how your relationship with money has been shaped by your experiences, including the impact of substance use. Through honest reflection, you can begin to understand past patterns, consider new perspectives, and take steps toward financial healing and stability.

Section 1: The Impact of Substance Use on Finances

1. How has substance use affected your finances (e.g., job loss, debt, legal fees, etc.)?

2. What financial consequences have been the most difficult for you to deal with?

3. Have you ever avoided or delayed facing financial problems? Why?

4. Are there financial decisions you regret that were influenced by your substance use?

Section 2: Messages About Money

1. What messages did you receive growing up about money (spoken or unspoken)?

2. Were you taught to save, spend, avoid, or fear money?

3. How do those early messages show up in your life today?

4. Do you want to keep or change any of those beliefs?

Section 3: Rebuilding Financial Health

1. What are some small financial goals you can set for yourself right now?

2. Who can support you in managing your money more effectively (e.g., peer support, financial coach, trusted friend)?

3. What tools or resources (e.g., budgeting apps, classes, support groups) might help you?

4. How can managing your finances support your recovery?

5. What is one action you can take this week to improve your financial wellness?

Section 4: Values and Financial Alignment

Consider how your financial decisions can align with your values in recovery.

1. What are some values that are important to you now (e.g., stability, honesty, growth)?

2. How can your money choices reflect these values?

3. What does financial integrity mean to you in this stage of your life?

Group Ten: Nutrition and Recovery

Group Ten: Nutrition and Recovery

Summary: Explore the role of nutrition in physical and emotional recovery.

Objectives:

- Understand how diet impacts mood and energy levels.
- Learn strategies for healthy eating.

References: "The Mood Cure" by Julia Ross.
Supplemental Reading: "Eat to Beat Depression and Anxiety" by Drew Ramsey.

How to Facilitate:

- Provide information on the link between nutrition and recovery.
- Share simple and affordable healthy eating tips.

Activities:

- Create a sample healthy meal plan.
- Discuss challenges to maintaining a healthy diet.

Clinician's Notes: Group Ten

Clinician's Notes: Group Ten

Clinician's Preparation & Core Knowledge

Group Ten explores how nutrition affects physical, emotional, and cognitive recovery. Many individuals in early recovery arrive with depleted nutrient reserves due to poor diet, chaotic lifestyles, or substance-related malabsorption. This group aims to educate clients on how food choices influence mood, energy, cravings, and treatment engagement.

Prepare by reviewing the relationship between nutrition and neurotransmitter function, particularly the roles of amino acids, omega-3s, and B-vitamins in supporting brain chemistry. Reinforce that this session is not about rigid diets or perfection, but about increasing awareness and offering small, achievable improvements.

Key sources include 'The Mood Cure' by Julia Ross and 'Eat to Beat Depression and Anxiety' by Drew Ramsey. Emphasize that dietary strategies should support—not replace—evidence-based mental health or addiction treatment.

Essential Talking Points for Clients

- *Restoring Neurochemical Balance:*
  Substance use often depletes essential nutrients critical for neurotransmitter production. Deficiencies in amino acids, B-vitamins, omega-3 fatty acids, and minerals like zinc and magnesium can impair mood regulation and increase relapse risk. Replenishing these nutrients supports the synthesis of serotonin, dopamine, and GABA, enhancing emotional stability and reducing cravings.

- *Improving Treatment Engagement and Outcomes:*
  Integrating nutrition education into SUD programs has been associated with better treatment outcomes. For instance, a study found that participants receiving nutrition education showed significant improvements in psychological and medical domains of the Addiction Severity Index (ASI). (Grant et al., 2004)

Engagement Tips to Make This Group Come Alive

- Start by asking: 'How do you feel when you haven't eaten well for a few days?' to connect nutrition with emotional state.

- Debunk myths: healthy eating doesn't have to be expensive, complicated, or extreme.

- Provide examples of mood-boosting foods (e.g., leafy greens, nuts, fish, legumes) and explain their role in brain function.

- Create a sample meal plan using simple, affordable ingredients. Encourage input and customization.

- Ask the group to identify barriers to healthy eating (e.g., money, time, knowledge) and brainstorm workarounds.

- Use handouts or visuals to explain how certain nutrients affect neurotransmitters and energy regulation.

Final Word to the Clinician

This session offers clients a powerful tool they can use daily to support their recovery. Normalize difficulty in changing food habits, and frame this not as another 'to-do,' but as a way to nourish both body and mind. Encourage clients to start with one small change and celebrate progress, not perfection.

Citations

Grant LP, Haughton B, Sachan DS. Nutrition education is positively associated with substance abuse treatment program outcomes. J Am Diet Assoc. 2004 Apr;104(4):604-10. doi: 10.1016/j.jada.2004.01.008. PMID: 15054346.

García-Estrada, J., et al. (2025). Malnutrition in Substance Use Disorders: A Critical Issue in Their Treatment and Recovery. Healthcare, 13(8), 868. https://doi.org/10.3390/healthcare13080868

Important Note

Important: Nutritional interventions should always complement, not replace, traditional treatments for depression, anxiety, and substance use disorders. Clients should consult with a qualified healthcare provider before making significant dietary changes. Clinicians are encouraged to partner with a licensed nutritionist for this module.

38

Healthy & Budget-Friendly Meal Planning

Group TEN: Worksheet One

Healthy & Budget-Friendly Meal Planning

This worksheet helps you create a healthy and affordable weekly meal plan. Use this tool to plan meals that support your physical health, emotional well-being, and recovery goals.

Section 1: What Makes a Meal Healthy?

A balanced meal typically includes:

- A source of protein (e.g., beans, chicken, tofu, eggs)
- Whole grains (e.g., brown rice, oats, whole wheat bread)
- Vegetables (fresh, frozen, or canned with low sodium)
- Fruits (fresh, frozen, or canned in juice)
- Healthy fats (e.g., olive oil, nuts, seeds, avocado)

Section 2: Budget-Friendly Food Ideas

- Canned beans, lentils, and chickpeas
- Brown rice, whole wheat pasta, oats
- Frozen vegetables and fruit
- Eggs, peanut butter, and canned tuna
- In-season produce or items on sale
- Store-brand items instead of name brands

Section 3: Weekly Meal Plan Template

Use the table below to write out your meals for the week.

Day	Breakfast	Lunch	Dinner
Monday			
Tuesday			
Wednesday			
Thursday			
Friday			
Saturday			
Sunday			

Section 4: Reflection Questions

1. How do you feel physically and emotionally when you eat nutritious meals?

2. What challenges do you face in eating healthy meals consistently?

3. What are some strategies to overcome those challenges (e.g., prepping ahead, finding sales)?

4. Who can support you in maintaining healthier eating habits?

5. What's one small change you can make this week in your food choices?

Group Eleven: Boundaries in Relationships

Group Eleven: Boundaries in Relationships

Summary: Teach clients how to set and maintain boundaries.

Objectives:
- Recognize the importance of boundaries in relationships.
- Learn techniques to establish and maintain boundaries.

References: "Boundaries" by Henry Cloud and John Townsend.
Supplemental Reading: "The Gifts of Imperfection" by Brené Brown.

How to Facilitate:

- Discuss the concept of boundaries and their role in healthy relationships.
- Provide examples of boundary-setting scenarios.

Activities:

- Practice role-playing boundary-setting conversations.
- Reflect on personal experiences with boundaries through journaling.

Clinician's Notes: Group Eleven

G roup Eleven: Boundaries

Clinician's Preparation & Core Knowledge

Group Eleven focuses on the role of boundaries in creating supportive, respectful, and sustainable relationships. Rather than framing boundaries as ways to shut others out, this session emphasizes boundaries as tools for clarifying personal values, needs, and comfort levels—especially during recovery when identity and priorities are shifting.

Familiarize yourself with the key concepts from 'Boundaries' by Henry Cloud and John Townsend, as well as Brené Brown's emphasis on vulnerability and self-respect. Understand that many clients may associate boundaries with guilt, conflict, or abandonment. Your role is to help reframe boundaries as acts of clarity and self-care—not rejection.

This topic can be emotionally charged. Normalize that learning to set boundaries is a process and that mistakes are part of the growth.

Essential Talking Points for Clients

- "Boundaries aren't about controlling others—they're about protecting your own well-being."
- "You get to decide what is and isn't okay for you—and communicate that clearly."
- "People may not always like your boundaries, but that doesn't make them wrong."
- "Clear boundaries help us build trust, safety, and honesty in relationships."

Engagement Tips to Make This Group Come Alive

- Start with a discussion: 'What comes to mind when you hear the word boundaries?' Normalize fear, discomfort, or past conflict.

- Break boundaries down into types: physical, emotional, time, energy, communication. Give real-life examples of each.

- Model a script: 'When you [behavior], I feel [emotion]. I need [boundary].' Then have the group try using it in pairs or small groups.

- Use journaling prompts like: 'A time I wish I had set a boundary was...' or 'One boundary I want to practice this week is...'

- Discuss respectful responses to boundary violations—what to do when others push back or ignore limits.

- Encourage clients to reflect on how boundaries support—not sabotage—connection, trust, and autonomy.

Final Word to the Clinician

Boundaries are not easy for most people—especially those recovering from trauma, people-pleasing, or enmeshment. This session may stir up grief or anger. Stay grounded, validate difficulty, and hold space for growth. Clients who begin to explore and assert boundaries often report greater peace, self-trust, and clarity in their relationships. Help them begin.

41

Boundary-Setting

Group ELEVEN: Worksheet One

Boundary-Setting: Supporting Your Recovery

Setting boundaries is an important part of recovery. Boundaries help protect your mental health, support your goals, and reduce stress from relationships that may not align with your values or needs. This worksheet will help you explore where boundaries are needed, how to set them, and how to create goals to follow through.

Section 1: Identify Relationships That May Need Boundaries

List the people or situations that consistently make it harder for you to maintain your recovery:
1. _____
2. _____
3. _____
4. _____

Section 2: Common Signs That Boundaries May Be Needed

- Feeling drained or resentful after interactions
- Being pressured to use substances or minimize recovery efforts
- Difficulty saying no or feeling guilty when you do
- Having your time, space, or priorities disrespected
- Feeling obligated to fix, rescue, or manage others' problems

Section 3: Examples of Boundaries You Can Set

- Limiting time spent with certain people
- Not allowing substance use around you
- Saying 'no' without overexplaining

- Leaving a situation that threatens your recovery
- Asking for space or time to yourself
-Being honest about your needs and feelings

Section 4: Action Steps to Set Boundaries

Think about the boundaries you want to set. What steps can you take to begin setting those boundaries?

Example: 'I will let my cousin know I can't hang out if she's been drinking.'

Boundary I need to set: _____

Action step I will take: _____

When I will do this: _____

What support I might need: _____

Section 5: Goals for Boundary Setting

Set realistic goals to practice setting and maintaining boundaries:

Short-Term Goal (this week): _____

Medium-Term Goal (this month): _____

Long-Term Goal (next 3 months): _____

Section 6: Reflection

1. How do you feel when someone respects your boundaries?
2. What has been hard about setting boundaries in the past?
3. How will boundary setting help support your recovery?
4. Who can help you stay accountable to your boundary goals?

Group Twelve: Understanding Shame and Guilt

Group Twelve: Understanding Shame and Guilt

Summary: Differentiate between shame and guilt and learn strategies to overcome them.

Objectives:

- Recognize the difference between shame and guilt.
- Develop coping strategies for managing these emotions.

References: "The Gifts of Imperfection" by Brené Brown.
Supplemental Reading: "Healing the Shame That Binds You" by John Bradshaw.

How to Facilitate:

- Discuss the definitions and impacts of shame and guilt.
- Facilitate a group discussion on personal experiences.

Activities:

- Write a letter of forgiveness to oneself.
- Practice self-compassion exercises.

Clinician's Notes: Group Twelve

Clinician's Preparation & Core Knowledge

Group Twelve helps clients explore two powerful emotional experiences—shame and guilt—and learn how to work through them in ways that support healing and accountability. Shame is often described as the feeling that 'I am bad,' while guilt reflects 'I did something bad.' This distinction is critical in recovery, where shame can fuel relapse, secrecy, and self-harm, while guilt can motivate positive change.

Review Brené Brown's research on vulnerability, shame resilience, and wholeheartedness, as well as John Bradshaw's exploration of developmental shame and internalized belief systems. Emphasize that shame grows in silence and secrecy, while healing begins in shared honesty and self-compassion.

Approach this topic with gentleness. Clients may disclose painful memories or beliefs—create a safe space, offer choices, and respect emotional boundaries.

Essential Talking Points for Clients

- "Guilt says 'I made a mistake.' Shame says 'I am the mistake.' Only one of these helps you grow."
- "You are not the worst thing you've ever done. Your past behavior doesn't cancel your worth."
- "Everyone has shame—but not everyone knows how to talk about it. That's what we're learning here."
- "Self-compassion doesn't mean letting yourself off the hook—it means healing so you can keep showing up."

Engagement Tips to Make This Group Come Alive

- Define shame vs. guilt and provide real-life recovery examples of each.

- Use visual metaphors—like carrying a heavy backpack of secrets—to help illustrate the emotional burden of shame.

- Model vulnerability by sharing a time (real or fictionalized) when guilt led to growth or shame created isolation.

- Offer a writing prompt: 'Dear Me, I forgive you for...' and allow clients to keep their letters private if they choose.

- Teach a simple self-compassion exercise: hand over heart, name a feeling, offer kindness ('This is hard. I'm doing my best.').

- Normalize resistance. Many people struggle with the idea of self-forgiveness. Let them go at their own pace.

Final Word to the Clinician

This session can be one of the most emotionally impactful. Shame is often deeply ingrained, and your job is to meet it with compassion, not confrontation. Let the group know they are not alone in these feelings—and that they are allowed to move forward, even if they're still healing. If clients begin to distinguish guilt from shame and take even a small step toward self-forgiveness, they've made meaningful progress.

44

Self-Forgiveness Letter

Group TWELVE: Worksheet One

Self-Forgiveness Letter

Forgiving yourself is a powerful act of healing. This worksheet is designed to help you reflect on your past, acknowledge your growth, and extend compassion to yourself. Writing a letter of self-forgiveness can be a meaningful step in your recovery process.

Writing Prompts

- What are some things you're holding against yourself from the past?
- How has your substance use or past behavior impacted how you view yourself?
- What would you say to a friend who went through something similar?
- What have you learned from your mistakes?
- What have you done to make things right or begin healing?
- Why do you deserve forgiveness?
- What will forgiveness free you to do moving forward?

Write Your Letter Below

Use the space below to write your letter. You can follow this structure or write freely from your heart

Dear Me,

[Acknowledge what you've been through. Talk about the choices you made, the pain you've carried, and what you want to let go of. Express understanding and kindness to yourself, and reflect on what you've learned. Offer forgiveness and support your continued growth.]

With compassion,

[Your Name]

Optional Reflection After Writing

    1. How did it feel to write this letter?
    2. What parts were hardest to write?
    3. What do you want to remember from this letter in the future?
    4. Would you like to keep this letter to read again later, or let it go as part of releasing the past?

Group Thirteen: Time Management

G roup Thirteen: Time Management

Summary: Teach clients the importance of effective time management in recovery.

Objectives:
- Understand the role of time management in reducing stress.
-Learn strategies to prioritize tasks and set goals.

References: "The 7 Habits of Highly Effective People" by Stephen Covey.
Supplemental Reading: "Atomic Habits" by James Clear.

How to Facilitate:
- Discuss common time management challenges in recovery.
-Provide practical tools such as to-do lists and scheduling.

Activities:
- Create a weekly schedule.
- Identify and discuss time-wasters and solutions.

Clinician's Notes: Group Thirteen

Clinician's Notes: Group Thirteen

Clinician's Preparation & Core Knowledge

Group Thirteen emphasizes time management as a recovery skill that promotes structure, reduces stress, and helps clients reconnect with their goals. Many people in early recovery struggle with under-scheduling (lack of structure) or over-committing (burnout), which can contribute to relapse risk or emotional overwhelm.

Familiarize yourself with Stephen Covey's principles of goal setting, prioritization, and values-driven action, as well as James Clear's practical strategies for habit formation. Help clients understand that effective time management isn't about control or rigidity—it's about intention and alignment.

Encourage realistic goal-setting. Many clients may feel overwhelmed by past disorganization or lost time. Start small and celebrate progress.

Essential Talking Points for Clients

- "Structure is one of the most powerful relapse prevention tools."
- "Time management isn't about being perfect—it's about making space for what really matters."
- "You can't manage time, but you can manage your energy and attention."
- "Small habits lead to big change—consistency beats intensity."

Engagement Tips to Make This Group Come Alive

- Begin with a discussion: 'How do you currently manage your time?' Normalize struggles with procrastination or chaos.
- Introduce a simple tool: a daily or weekly planner, a to-do list, or time-blocking chart.

- Facilitate a values clarification: What do you want to make more time for in your life (e.g., family, health, creativity)?

- Have clients build a sample weekly schedule including work, rest, recovery activities, meals, and fun.

- Discuss common time-wasters (e.g., doom-scrolling, overcommitting, avoidance) and brainstorm solutions.

- Introduce the 2-minute rule: if a task takes less than two minutes, do it now.

Final Word to the Clinician

Time management isn't about fixing people—it's about helping them build rhythm and focus in their lives. Clients in recovery are often rebuilding routines from scratch. Be patient, encouraging, and flexible. Help them see that each hour they spend with intention is a win—and a step toward a more grounded, purposeful future.

47

Weekly Schedule Planning

Group THIRTEEN: Worksheet One

Weekly Schedule Planning

Creating a consistent weekly schedule helps support structure, reduce stress, and reinforce your recovery goals. Use this worksheet to map out your week, include healthy habits, and plan time for rest, work, connection, and support.

Instructions:

1. Begin by filling in any fixed commitments (work, appointments, groups).
2. Schedule self-care activities (sleep, meals, exercise, relaxation).
3. Add in recovery supports (meetings, therapy, check-ins).
4. Plan time for things that bring you joy or a sense of purpose.
5. Keep room for flexibility, but aim for consistency.

Reflection Before You Begin:

1. What do you need more of in your week? _____
2. What do you want to make time for that you haven't been? _____
3. When do you feel most vulnerable or at risk? What supports can go there? _____

Weekly Schedule Template

Day	Morning	Afternoon	Evening
Monday			
Tuesday			
Wednesday			
Thursday			
Friday			
Saturday			
Sunday			

End of Week Reflection:

1. What worked well this week about your schedule?
2. What was difficult or didn't work as planned?
3. What will you adjust for next week to better support your goals?

48

Values and Time Alignment

Group THIRTEEN: Worksheet Two

Values and Time Alignment

Living a life aligned with your values helps you build purpose, direction, and meaning in recovery. This worksheet will help you identify your core values, reflect on how you currently spend your time, and plan for changes that bring you closer to the life you want.

Step 1: Identify Your Core Values

Review the list below and circle or highlight the values that matter most to you. Then, choose your top five values.

Family, Friendship, Honesty, Growth, Stability, Freedom, Spirituality, Compassion, Creativity, Respect, Health, Kindness, Adventure, Purpose, Justice, Humor, Independence, Education, Peace, Resilience, Recovery, Balance, Achievement, Self-Respect, Community, Gratitude

Top 5 values:

1. _____
2. _____
3. _____
4. _____
5. _____

Step 2: How Do You Spend Your Time?

List how you typically spend your time in a day or week (e.g., work, sleep, social media, meetings, chores):

What activities support your top values?

What activities do not align with your values or leave you feeling drained?

Step 3: Bridge the Gap Between Values and Time

What small changes can you make to spend more time on what matters most to you?

What boundaries or limits might you set to reduce time spent on distractions or habits that don't support your values?

List 3 goals to help you align your time with your values:
1.

_____

2.

_____

3.

_____

49

Supplemental Group: The Power of Support Networks

Supplemental Group: The Power of Support Networks

Summary:
Explore the role of social connection and support—both informal and formal, including peer support groups—in fostering resilience and sustaining long-term recovery.

Objectives:

- Understand how healthy relationships support recovery outcomes.
- Identify the elements of a strong support network.
- Explore different forms of peer support (e.g., AA, NA, SMART Recovery, recovery coaches).
- Develop a plan to build or strengthen a recovery-oriented social system.

Supplemental Reading:
The Connected Life: The Art and Science of Relational Healing by Todd W. Hall

How to Facilitate:

- Introduce the idea of "recovery capital" and social support as a form of it.
- Present examples of different kinds of support networks (family, friends, sponsors, support groups, faith communities).
- Discuss myths and fears about asking for help.
- Normalize the awkwardness of rebuilding relationships.

Activities:

- Have participants map their current support system (Support Network Map worksheet).

- Small group discussions: "When have you felt supported, and how did it affect your recovery?"
- Role-play asking for help or setting up a boundary with a loved one.
- Brainstorm ways to strengthen or expand their support network.

50

Support Network Map

SUPPLEMENTAL Group: Worksheet One

Support Network Map

Building a support network is a powerful part of recovery. This worksheet helps you identify who is in your support network, the roles they play, and who you might want to connect with more intentionally. Use the diagram area to visually map out your support system.

Instructions:

Start by writing your name in the center of a circle you will draw below. Then add the names of people, groups, or organizations that support you around that circle. Use the sections provided to reflect on who supports you emotionally, practically, and in your recovery journey.

My Circle of Support

Emotional Support

Who can you talk to when you're feeling overwhelmed, sad, or joyful?

How often do you connect with these people? _____

Practical Support

Who helps you with tasks, appointments, rides, childcare, or other day-to-day needs?

Recovery Support

Who helps support your sobriety or healing? (e.g., sponsor, peer support, therapist, group)

Areas to Grow or Strengthen

Are there people you want to connect with more? _____

Are there types of support you are missing or want to seek out? _____

51

Supplemental Group: Parenting in Early Recovery

Supplemental Group: Parenting in Early Recovery

Summary:
Support parents in navigating the challenges of parenting while managing their own recovery, with a focus on realistic expectations, emotional availability, and healing family systems.

Objectives:

- Identify common challenges of parenting during early recovery.
- Explore guilt, shame, and trauma in the parent-child relationship.
- Learn strategies to stay emotionally present and manage stress.
- Set developmentally appropriate parenting goals.

References:
Parenting with Love and Logic by Cline & Fay
Supplemental Reading:
The Whole-Brain Child by Dan Siegel and Tina Payne Bryson

How to Facilitate:

- Begin with normalization: Parenting is hard *even without* early recovery.
- Use guided discussion around emotional regulation, parental guilt, and rebuilding trust.
- Present brain science around how kids co-regulate with their caregivers.
- Introduce basic parenting frameworks that emphasize structure *and* nurture.

Activities:

- Have clients journal on "What kind of parent do I want to be?" and "What gets in the way?"

• Create a parenting values chart (e.g., patience, presence, honesty).
• Practice repair conversations through role-play.
• Group brainstorm: "What helps you stay present with your children during hard days?"

52

Parenting and Recovery

S UPPLEMENTAL Group: Worksheet Two

Parenting and Recovery

Parenting in recovery means rediscovering the parent you want to be—without substances interfering. This worksheet will help you explore your parenting values, reflect on how substance use has impacted your relationship with your child(ren), and set realistic goals to grow in your role as a caregiver.

Step 1: Define Your Parenting Values

Check or circle the values that are important to you as a parent:

Consistency, Patience, Empathy, Structure, Safety, Love, Responsibility, Communication, Honesty, Respect, Playfulness, Boundaries, Being Present, Teaching, Protection, Support, Trust, Stability, Creativity, Calmness

My top 3 parenting values are:
1. _____
2. _____
3. _____

Step 2: Reflection on Substance Use

How has substance use affected your ability to parent the way you want to?

What are some moments you wish could have gone differently?

Step 3: Parenting Without Substance Use

Imagine parenting without the influence of substances:

What would be different about your relationship with your child(ren)?

What kind of role model would you like to be?

Step 4: Setting Recovery-Based Parenting Goals

Write three realistic goals to help you be the parent you want to be:

1. _____
2. _____
3. _____

Who can support you in achieving these parenting goals? _____

53

References/Citations

R eferences

Bowen, S., Chawla, N., & Marlatt, G. A. (2011). *Mindfulness-based relapse prevention for addictive behaviors: A clinician's guide.* Guilford Press.

Bradberry, T., & Greaves, J. (2009). *Emotional intelligence 2.0.* TalentSmart.

Bradshaw, J. (2005). *Healing the shame that binds you.* Health Communications, Inc.

Brown, B. (2010). *The gifts of imperfection: Let go of who you think you're supposed to be and embrace who you are.* Hazelden Publishing.

Clear, J. (2018). *Atomic habits: An easy & proven way to build good habits & break bad ones.* Avery.

Cline, F., & Fay, J. (2006). *Parenting with love and logic: Teaching children responsibility.* NavPress.

Covey, S. R. (1989). *The 7 habits of highly effective people: Powerful lessons in personal change.* Free Press.

García-Estrada, J., Luquin, S., Pesqueda-Cendejas, K., Ruiz-Ballesteros, A. I., Campos-López, B., Meza-Meza, M. R., Parra-Rojas, I., González-Castañeda, R. E., Ramos-Lopez, O., & De la Cruz-Mosso, U. (2025). Malnutrition in substance use disorders: A critical issue in their treatment and recovery. *Healthcare, 13*(8), 868. https://doi.org/10.3390/healthcare13080868

Gorski, T. T. (1989). Staying sober: A guide for relapse prevention. Herald Publishing House.

Gottman, J. M., & Silver, N. (1999). *The seven principles for making marriage work*. Crown Publishing Group.

Grant, L. P., Haughton, B., & Sachan, D. S. (2004). Nutrition education is positively associated with substance abuse treatment program outcomes. *Journal of the American Dietetic Association, 104* (4), 604–610. https://doi.org/10.1016/j.jada.2004.01.008

Hay, L. (1984). *You can heal your life*. Hay House, Inc.

Kabat-Zinn, J. (2005). *Wherever you go, there you are: Mindfulness meditation in everyday life*. Hachette Books.

Levine, A., & Heller, R. S. (2010). *Attached: The new science of adult attachment and how it can help you find—and keep—love*. TarcherPerigee.

Linehan, M. M. (2015). *DBT skills training manual* (2nd ed.). Guilford Press.

Maté, G. (2010). *In the realm of hungry ghosts: Close encounters with addiction*. North Atlantic Books.

McKay, M., Wood, J. C., & Brantley, J. (2007). *The dialectical behavior therapy skills workbook: Practical DBT exercises for learning mindfulness, interpersonal effectiveness, emotion regulation, and distress tolerance*. New Harbinger Publications.

Meyers, R. J., & Wolfe, B. L. (2004). *Get your loved one sober: Alternatives to nagging, pleading, and threatening*. Hazelden Publishing.

Peltz, L. (2013). *The mindful path to addiction recovery: A practical guide to regaining control over your life*. Trumpeter.

Ramsey, D. (2009). *The total money makeover: A proven plan for financial fitness*. Thomas Nelson.

Robin, V., & Dominguez, J. (2008). *Your money or your life: 9 steps to transforming your relationship with money and achieving financial independence*. Penguin.

Ross, J. (2004). *The mood cure: The 4-step program to take charge of your emotions—today*. Penguin.

Schiraldi, G. R. (2001). *The self-esteem workbook*. New Harbinger Publications.

Townsend, J. S., & Cloud, H. (1992). *Boundaries: When to say yes, how to say no to take control of your life.* Zondervan.

Carmichael Finn, MA, LMFT, LADC, ADCR-MN, is an experienced therapist, educator, and behavioral health leader dedicated to advancing ethical, trauma-informed care in substance use disorder treatment. As the Executive Director of Recovering Hope Treatment Center in Minnesota, Carmichael oversees residential and outpatient programs serving families, and he is a tireless advocate for dignity, justice, and access within the behavioral health system.

Carmichael is also the founder of **Carmichael Finn LLC**, through which he trains and consults on clinical supervision, ethics, and systemic accountability in mental health and addiction services. He holds dual licensure as a Licensed Marriage and Family Therapist and Licensed Alcohol and Drug Counselor, and he teaches at colleges, mentoring the next generation of helping professionals.

Drawing on years of direct practice, leadership experience, and training, Carmichael creates tools like this workbook to bring depth, structure, and heart into the recovery process. His approach is rooted in harm reduction, relational healing, and a deep belief that every person deserves the chance to recover with support, self-respect, and community.

For training inquiries or speaking engagements, visit www.carmichaelfinn.com